MW01283342

I'M RETIRED. NOW WHAT?

CHOOSING TO LIVE A HAPPY AND PURPOSEFUL RETIREMENT LIFE - BOOK AND WEEKLY JOURNAL

RUSTY ELLIS

SHADY PINES
- PRESS -

CONTENTS

FOREWORD

Whoever said retirement would be easy...was a genius! I can't lie, retirement is great. Or for many, could be great. This book *isn't* focused on your finances or how to financial prepare for retirement. It *is* about what can make out of your retirement years.

One thing I've found about retirement is that without a certain level of focus, you can lose track of the days, weeks, and even months, with nothing to show for them. And that's, well, just simply sad.

You just finished with a career where you were relied upon as a member of a team. You produced something to be compensated for your work, then just like that, you woke up the day after retirement and it was gone. The things which used to be relegated to the evenings and weekends are not the main focus of your life, and now you have more time to focus on them. The excuse of "not enough time" is gone. If all you are accomplishing now is keeping the local cable company in business, and wearing out batteries in your TV remote, you're not doing retirement right!

You've spent decades of your life gaining insight and wisdom. You've become an expert in areas through trial and error or through education and training—more than likely all of the above. Either way, you're smarter than you were when you started your journey here on earth. And now you have the opportunity to continue to grow, continue to give back, continue to develop strong relationships, and leave a legacy worth smiling about.

So let's get started!

SURVIVE OR THRIVE

I 'm a fan of the word "Opine."

Opine: (verb) hold and state as one's opinion: [with direct speech] : "The man is a genius," he opined | [with clause] : the critic opined that the most exciting musical moment occurred when the orchestra struck up the national anthem.

And with that, I shall now *opine*...

I was discussing life "post-50-years-old" with a friend of mine. We talked about how we spend our time and came up with an interesting consensus. Our first 50 years of life seemed as though we had time to spare, time to waste, time to trample, time to cast off...you get the gist.

Post-50 seems different. My time seems a little more, well, borrowed. You can't argue if you put your life on a bell curve 50 would be somewhere toward the peak (hopefully!). Now I'm on the downhill slope. My time feels more precious to me. I think more about where I'm spending it and if it's worthy of the investment.

Don't get me wrong. Some things are just flat-out fun and should be enjoyed. But I would just argue you need to make sure they are worthy of the investment. Two things come to mind right off: television and internet.

One thing I've discovered about myself as of late is my need for information. Being entertained is important as well, but I select my entertainment, not the other way around.

When I sit down to watch something on television, I generally have an idea of what I'm going to watch. I'd like to think I've matured beyond the "surf the channels and watch the best of the worst" days of my life. Prime example, college football. This sport is purely for enjoyment and something I'm willing to donate my time to. However, due to the amazing addition of technology, I can record a game and watch it at a time when it doesn't interfere with more important things (ie. family time, date with wife). See? I'm not saying to abandon entertainment. I'm just saying it's important to lucidly decide on how it fits into your life.

Okay, opine over (mostly).

The next five sections of the book will cover key areas of your life, with a smidgeon of opining:

1. Personal
2. Health
3. Spiritual
4. Family
(Relationships)
5. Financial

ONE

PERSONAL GROWTH

S tarting the Personal Growth section reminds me of two things:

> 1) *Some can view the word personal as being selfish*
> 2) *you can't save others if you are drowning too.*

Not meaning to be a harsh start to this section, but the importance of taking care of the personal side of you is critical in being mentally and physically available for the other areas of your life where you can make a difference. Agreed? **Agreed!**

We break down parts of the personal section into several different groups as we progress through the chapters of this book. However, we will touch on "the personal you" here first. Outside of Health and Spiritual, there is you as an educated and ever growing person.

There is no holding still in life, no great pause button, no just "give me a minute" to take a breath. Either you're Surviving or Thriving. And as we get older, the last thing we want to do is choose to Survive. Admittedly, Surviving is something your body and mind will want to do without your active input. Thriving takes an active approach to fight against the natural gravity of life.

How do you choose to Thrive? How are you moving forward and kicking gravity to the curb?

One of the first things you can do is step back and evaluate your day. Evaluate what takes up your time each day. Yes, everything.

- Television
- Social Media
- Reading
- Music
- Telephone
- Exercise
- Church
- Travel
- ...and the list goes on.

So when you're lying in bed at night, and reviewing what you accomplished, did you dictate your life or did your life dictate you? Did you start your day with a plan or did the day plan it for you as it went?

One thing I've found is my mental health breaths of sigh of relief when I get to the end of the day and can look back and see what I've accomplished. Another biggie is watching a college football game and knowing I've accomplished the things on my list. Not that I need to earn it, but it feels good to watch the game knowing my todo items made it into the to-done category for the day.

Did you evaluate your day? Did you make a plan for the day?

TWO

HEALTH

L et me set the stage...
We've been taught all our lives—especially our genera-
tion—to improve upon everything we do. When I was about 45
years old, I woke up at 3 a.m. during the week to go to the gym.
Part of it was my health and part of it was to battle my eating
condition (I love to eat!). Bonus: A couple of my kids even got up
and joined me in the morning.

One of my goals at the gym was to work up to a 300-pound
benchpress. I worked hard at it and was encouraged by my sons
along the way. I spent each day at the gym to improve and focus
on this goal. The side effects were brutal at times, with my
elbows being so tender that I couldn't rest them on the table. But
I was committed to this goal.

Well, it didn't happen. For the record, the best I could do was

298 pounds. My elbows just couldn't take any more. Did I fail? Yes and no.

I didn't hit the "Big 300" but my sons were forever impressed with my efforts. And sometimes, just having your kids proud of you is enough.

The battle now is knowing I need to exercise, but changing my goals to match my life and health. I had to change my goals to something which complimented where my body is in life *now* and gave me the best shot at extending my life as healthily as possible.

So what does exercise and a good workout look like to you? Only you can answer that question. Again, you have to weigh where you're at in life physically against your overall goals.

"A lot of the symptoms that we associate with old age—such as weakness and loss of balance—are actually symptoms of inactivity, not age..." - Alicia I. Arbaje, MD, MPH, assistant professor of Geriatrics and Gerontology at Johns Hopkins University School of Medicine in Baltimore.

Your exercise could range from going to the gym and doing cardio followed by lifting weights, to going for a walk around your neighborhood, to performing exercises in a chair to maintain mobility. You know you and your limitations. You need to commit to exercise in a way best suiting your situation. And just as important, make it an attainable goal and habit.

One thing I've noticed about exercise is the effect it has on my mental health. Without going into the whole, "when you exercise, your body releases endorphins which..." blah-blah-blah; let's just say you feel great!

Even being sore the next day can feel good in a little bit of a twisted way. The pain reminds you of the physical investment you made in yourself. The little aches and pains from exercise should give you the thought of, "Oh yea, I can do this!" Pat yourself on the back, but don't strain your arm. That's a different kind of hurt we can do without.

My suggestion to you for exercise? Let's start with, "I'm not a doctor. Consult your doctor before starting any new exercise regimen." There, the lawyer-stuff is out of the way. My suggestion is choose something you enjoy doing and make it a habit. Ground breaking, right?!?

As I said earlier, whether you are hitting the gym or strolling around your neighborhood, do what's healthy for you and...**DO IT!**

Make it a habit. Enjoy the physical and mental benefits stemming from exercise. And in addition to the next four sections we'll discuss—be a role model to your friends and family!

Already doing this? Bravo, bravo my friend. Keep it up!

THREE

SPIRITUAL

T his chapter is not a crash-course in religion. I'm not going to tell you how, or when, or why your Spiritual component needs to be addressed...okay, maybe a little. Just so you can get a little perspective as to how I think it's important in balancing your life and especially your retirement life.

I recently took an online calendar and changed the days of the week on it. It was a monthly calendar, with a row across the top reading each day of the week. I changed it to read:

SATURDAY | SATURDAY | SATURDAY | SATURDAY | SATURDAY | SATURDAY | SUNDAY

Get it? Come on, look again. Now do you get it? Of course you do. It's a retirement calendar!

I thought it was genius. I posted it up to my friends on a social media site and they went bonkers. Not good bonkers. More like, "not fair" and "jerk" bonkers. Yeah, that kind of bonkers. Well, I thought it was funny.

The reason I brought this up—other than to give you a good laugh—is to mention the importance of my Spiritual Day to me. Not only is it a day for me to set aside and recognize as different from the rest of the week, it's also my weekly reset. It's a great placeholder for getting a Birdseye View of the upcoming week and do some planning. It's literally my reset day so everyday isn't a Saturday.

Is everyday a Saturday a bad thing? Depends on who you ask. If college football was on everyday—remember, every day being Saturday—then no, it would be great. Opposing position: my wife. She would argue against college football every day and prefers a reset day as well.

Is a Spiritual Day important?

You can take your Spiritual Day in any direction you choose. I just think it's a good day to consider things we normally take for granted each week. It's a good day to give yourself permission to break from the normal monotony of the week. Whether you attend formal church services or choose to meditate at home, a Spiritual Day is an important element to your long-term retirement lifestyle (IMHO).

May I add, two words come to mind specifically in relation to this day. You can incorporate them during the week, and probably should. The words are: Selflessness and Gratitude.

Between having a Spiritual Day, and keeping Selflessness and Gratitude in mind, doing a little something each day toward the latter two will add more substance and meaning to your life. Guaranteed!

There, do with them what you will, but do something with them. Good job. Okay, done with my spiritual opining.

FOUR

FAMILY (RELATIONSHIPS)

Where do you get your greatest ideas about life? Me? In the shower of course. The one place where I don't have the ability to write things down. I've half considered putting a chalkboard in the shower, but you can already see where that would fail (shrug).

Usually after having a breakthrough idea or thought in the shower, I rush to my bedroom and dictate the idea on my cellphone. The latest idea was a little morbid. But, it fits right here when talking about family. I call it, "Reverse Funeral Engineering."

It goes something like this:

Close your eyes and picture yourself at your own funeral.
Got it? Good. Now look around and see who you'd expect

13

to be attending. Is anyone missing? Go ahead, add them, after all, this is your funeral.

Now let's Reverse Funeral Engineer it. Write down a list of the people at the funeral. This list could include family, friends, former co-workers, and anyone else having meaning in your life. Done? Let's move on.

Have you had contact with the people on the list recently. Have you seen, called, texted, or sent a note/letter to them? Yes? Awesome. No? Then why should they come to your funeral?

Really. Yes, this is a little harsh. If they mean enough to you to have them at your funeral, shouldn't they mean enough to contact before then?

It's kind of like what my dental hygienist told me at my last visit for a teeth cleaning.

"Do you floss?" she asked.

"Why, of course," I responded.

"You know, you only have to floss the teeth you want to keep."

It took me a minute to realize what she was telling me...just like it's taking you a minute as well. Her point. Only give attention to the teeth you want to keep. Same with relationships. If you want to keep them around, you need to give them some sort of attention.

Two more thoughts about this. We live in an era where communication is ridiculously easy. Sending a text or email to someone is an easy way to engage someone with a "just thinking about you" comment. Go ahead, try it!

The second thought. This relates a little back to the Spiritual chapter. When someone comes to mind, drop them a line. They may be coming to mind because they need a little boost. Have you ever received a quick note or text from someone out of the blue? Did it make you mad? Or did it make your day? Exactly. There you go.

FIVE

FINANCIAL

There are three levels of retirement:

- Retired - Your income is covering you and you aren't working to cover the bills.
- Semi-Retired - Working a part-time job while receiving a retirement income.
- Working - You could be receiving a retirement income but are working full-time.

I'm blessed to be the first guy. I'm not planning any trips to luxurious island locations in the near future, but I'm also not eating Top Ramen three meals a day (full disclosure: I love Top Ramen. Wife won't let me eat it for every meal).

Let me share an interesting discussion I had just before I retired with my Finance Guy. I love saying that I have a Finance

Guy. He's the guy that says "nope" when I want to take a larger monthly chunk of money out of my account...kind of like my wife (Sorry, I digress).

When we went over my retirement figures and my plans for retirement, he actually got excited, "I'm relieved you have a realistic view of what your retirement looks like with the money you've saved."

Again, I can plan a few trips here and there, I'm a pretty cheap date (or so the wife says). But my trips are usually focused around seeing family. Just my choice. Just my focus. If I want to take a wham-bang blowout vacation tour of Europe, well, I'm going to need to sell my motorcycle or get a job. Reality. But you know what, if the other areas of your life are pretty squared away, then it gives you a different view of what you "want" and more importantly, what you "need."

I guess what I'm saying here is live within your means. We want our kids to do this, so we should set the example for them. Figure your budget and live accordingly. Cut back in areas where you need to enjoy things of more importance. I think Confucius referred to this as "Common Sense." Yeah, that.

AFTERWORD

The next pages in this book provide you with a weekly planner for the upcoming year. You can use this for a number of different things, from keeping appointments to jotting down ideas. It's also a great place to write down what you've accomplished for the day and even to create you own little gratitude journal. It's yours, so go crazy!

The daily areas we covered in this book:

- Plan Your Day
- Personal
- Exercise
- Spiritual (Selflessness and Gratitude)
- Family (Relationships)
- Financial
- Evaluate Your Day

The challenge is pulling it all together, making all the pieces to the puzzle come together, without missing a piece. Can you do it? Yes, yes you can!

ABOUT THE AUTHOR

Rusty Ellis is the eldest of seven children born to Paul and Shari Ellis. He grew up living in a number of different cities, due to his father's career in the U.S. Air Force. Rusty has lived in California (where he was born), Utah, Florida, Alaska, Virginia, Idaho, Wyoming, and in Las Vegas, Nevada, where he now resides.

Rusty met his wife in Rexburg, Idaho, while attending college. The two were married a short time after (six months later!) and have continued to date and court to this day. Rusty and DaLea have six children, five daughters-in-law, one son-in-law, and eight grandchildren (with two more on the way).

DaLea is employed as a Realtor and Rusty retired from active law enforcement duty in 2018.

Rusty wrote his first book in 2005, The Blank Slate. He is currently working on a Crime Series around his character Ransom Walsh.

Rusty enjoys spending time with his family, his two dogs, hunting deer with his friends, and riding his Victory motorcycle.

facebook.com/rustyellisauthor

twitter.com/RustyEllisNV

instagram.com/rustyellisnv

amazon.com/author/rustyellis

goodreads.com/rustyellis

pinterest.com/rustyellisnv

bookbub.com/profile/rusty-ellis

WEEKLY PLANNER/JOURNAL PAGES

Month/Year: _____

_____TO_____

○ MONDAY

PRIORITIES

_____

_____

_____

○ TUESDAY

_____

_____

_____

_____

○ WEDNESDAY

TO DO

_____

_____

○ THURSDAY

_____

_____

_____

_____

○ FRIDAY

_____

_____

_____

_____

○ SATURDAY / SUNDAY

_____

_____

_____

_____

Month/Year: _____

___ Plan Your Day
___ Personal
___ Exercise
___ Spiritual
___ Family
___ Financial
___ Evaluate Your Day

_____TO_____

○ MONDAY

PRIORITIES

_____

_____

○ TUESDAY

_____

_____

_____

_____

○ WEDNESDAY

TO DO

_____

_____

○ THURSDAY

_____

_____

_____

_____

○ FRIDAY

_____

_____

_____

_____

○ SATURDAY / SUNDAY

_____

_____

_____

Month/Year: _____

_____TO_____

○ MONDAY

PRIORITIES

_____

○ TUESDAY

_____

_____

_____

_____

○ WEDNESDAY

TO DO

_____

○ THURSDAY

_____

_____

_____

_____

○ FRIDAY

_____

_____

_____

○ SATURDAY / SUNDAY

_____

_____

_____

Month/Year: _____

__ Plan Your Day
__ Personal
__ Exercise
__ Spiritual
__ Family
__ Financial
__ Evaluate Your Day

_____TO_____

○ MONDAY

PRIORITIES

_____

_____

○ TUESDAY

_____

_____

_____

○ WEDNESDAY

TO DO

_____

○ THURSDAY

_____

_____

_____

_____

○ FRIDAY

_____

_____

_____

_____

○ SATURDAY / SUNDAY

_____

_____

_____

Month/Year: _____

___ Plan Your Day
___ Personal
___ Exercise
___ Spiritual
___ Family
___ Financial
___ Evaluate Your Day

_____TO_____

○ MONDAY

PRIORITIES

_____

_____

○ TUESDAY

_____

_____

_____

○ WEDNESDAY

TO DO

_____

○ THURSDAY

_____

_____

_____

○ FRIDAY

_____

_____

_____

_____

○ SATURDAY / SUNDAY

_____

_____

_____

_____

Month/Year: _____

___ Plan Your Day
___ Personal
___ Exercise
___ Spiritual
___ Family
___ Financial
___ Evaluate Your Day

_____TO_____

○ MONDAY

PRIORITIES

_____

_____

_____

○ TUESDAY

_____

_____

_____

_____

○ WEDNESDAY

TO DO

_____

_____

○ THURSDAY

_____

_____

_____

_____

○ FRIDAY

_____

_____

_____

○ SATURDAY / SUNDAY

_____

_____

_____

Month/Year: _____

_____TO_____

○ MONDAY

_____

PRIORITIES

_____
_____
○ TUESDAY
_____
_____
_____
_____
_____
○ WEDNESDAY

TO DO

_____
_____
○ THURSDAY
_____
_____
_____
_____
_____
○ FRIDAY
_____
_____
_____
_____
○ SATURDAY / SUNDAY
_____
_____
_____
_____

Month/Year: _____

_____TO_____

○ MONDAY

PRIORITIES

_____

○ TUESDAY

_____

○ WEDNESDAY

TO DO

_____

○ THURSDAY

_____

○ FRIDAY

_____

○ SATURDAY / SUNDAY

Month/Year: _____

_____TO_____

○ MONDAY

PRIORITIES

_____

_____

○ TUESDAY

_____

_____

_____

_____

_____

○ WEDNESDAY

TO DO

_____

_____

○ THURSDAY

_____

_____

_____

_____

○ FRIDAY

_____

_____

_____

_____

○ SATURDAY / SUNDAY

_____

_____

_____

_____

Month/Year: _____

__ Plan Your Day
__ Personal
__ Exercise
__ Spiritual
__ Family
__ Financial
__ Evaluate Your Day

_____TO_____

○ MONDAY

PRIORITIES

_____

_____

○ TUESDAY

_____

_____

_____

_____

○ WEDNESDAY

TO DO

_____

_____

○ THURSDAY

_____

_____

_____

○ FRIDAY

_____

_____

_____

_____

○ SATURDAY / SUNDAY

_____

_____

_____

Month/Year: _____

__ Plan Your Day
__ Personal
__ Exercise
__ Spiritual
__ Family
__ Financial
__ Evaluate Your Day

_____TO_____

○ MONDAY

PRIORITIES

_____

_____

○ TUESDAY

_____

_____

_____

_____

_____

_____

○ WEDNESDAY

TO DO

_____

_____

_____

○ THURSDAY

_____

_____

_____

_____

_____

_____

○ FRIDAY

_____

_____

_____

_____

_____

○ SATURDAY / SUNDAY

_____

_____

_____

_____

_____

Month/Year: _____

___ Plan Your Day

___ Plan Your Day
___ Personal
___ Exercise
___ Spiritual
___ Family
___ Financial
___ Evaluate Your Day

_____TO_____

○ MONDAY

PRIORITIES

_____

○ TUESDAY

_____

_____

_____

_____

○ WEDNESDAY

TO DO

_____

_____

○ THURSDAY

_____

_____

_____

_____

○ FRIDAY

_____

_____

_____

○ SATURDAY / SUNDAY

_____

_____

_____

Month/Year: _____

_____TO_____

○ MONDAY

PRIORITIES

_____

○ TUESDAY

_____

○ WEDNESDAY

TO DO

_____

○ THURSDAY

_____

○ FRIDAY

_____

○ SATURDAY / SUNDAY

_____

Month/Year: _____

__ Plan Your Day
__ Personal
__ Exercise
__ Spiritual
__ Family
__ Financial
__ Evaluate Your Day

_____TO_____

○ MONDAY

PRIORITIES

_____

_____

○ TUESDAY

_____

_____

_____

_____

○ WEDNESDAY

TO DO

_____

_____

○ THURSDAY

_____

_____

_____

_____

○ FRIDAY

_____

_____

_____

_____

○ SATURDAY / SUNDAY

_____

_____

_____

_____

Month/Year: _____

_____TO_____

○ MONDAY

PRIORITIES

_____

○ TUESDAY

_____

_____

_____

_____

○ WEDNESDAY

TO DO

_____

○ THURSDAY

_____

_____

_____

○ FRIDAY

_____

_____

_____

○ SATURDAY / SUNDAY

_____

_____

_____

Month/Year: _____

__ Plan Your Day
__ Personal
__ Exercise
__ Spiritual
__ Family
__ Financial
__ Evaluate Your Day

_____TO_____

○ MONDAY

PRIORITIES

_____

_____

○ TUESDAY

_____

_____

_____

_____

○ WEDNESDAY

TO DO

_____

_____

○ THURSDAY

_____

_____

_____

_____

○ FRIDAY

_____

_____

_____

○ SATURDAY / SUNDAY

_____

_____

_____

_____

Month/Year: _____

__ Plan Your Day
__ Personal
__ Exercise
__ Spiritual
__ Family
__ Financial
__ Evaluate Your Day

_____TO_____

○ MONDAY

PRIORITIES

_____

_____

○ TUESDAY

_____

_____

_____

_____

○ WEDNESDAY

TO DO

_____

_____

○ THURSDAY

_____

_____

_____

_____

○ FRIDAY

_____

_____

_____

_____

○ SATURDAY / SUNDAY

_____

_____

_____

Month/Year: _____

___ Plan Your Day
___ Personal
___ Exercise
___ Spiritual
___ Family
___ Financial
___ Evaluate Your Day

_____TO_____

○ MONDAY

PRIORITIES

_____

○ TUESDAY

_____

_____

_____

_____

○ WEDNESDAY

TO DO

_____

○ THURSDAY

_____

_____

_____

_____

○ FRIDAY

_____

_____

_____

_____

○ SATURDAY / SUNDAY

_____

_____

_____

_____

Month/Year: _____

_____TO_____

○ MONDAY

PRIORITIES

_____

_____

_____

○ TUESDAY

_____

_____

_____

_____

○ WEDNESDAY

TO DO

_____

_____

○ THURSDAY

_____

_____

_____

_____

○ FRIDAY

_____

_____

_____

○ SATURDAY / SUNDAY

_____

_____

_____

Month/Year: _____

_____TO_____

○ MONDAY

PRIORITIES

_____

○ TUESDAY

○ WEDNESDAY

TO DO

○ THURSDAY

○ FRIDAY

○ SATURDAY / SUNDAY

Month/Year: _____

_____TO_____

○ MONDAY

PRIORITIES

_____

_____

○ TUESDAY

_____

_____

_____

_____

○ WEDNESDAY

TO DO

_____

_____

○ THURSDAY

_____

_____

_____

_____

○ FRIDAY

_____

_____

_____

○ SATURDAY / SUNDAY

_____

_____

_____

Month/Year: _____

_____TO_____

__ Plan Your Day
__ Personal
__ Exercise
__ Spiritual
__ Family
__ Financial
__ Evaluate Your Day

○ MONDAY

PRIORITIES

_____

_____

○ TUESDAY

_____

_____

_____

○ WEDNESDAY

TO DO

_____

_____

○ THURSDAY

_____

_____

_____

_____

○ FRIDAY

_____

_____

_____

○ SATURDAY / SUNDAY

_____

_____

_____

_____

Month/Year: _____

__ Plan Your Day
__ Personal
__ Exercise
__ Spiritual
__ Family
__ Financial
__ Evaluate Your Day

_____TO_____

○ MONDAY

PRIORITIES

_____

_____

○ TUESDAY

_____

_____

_____

_____

○ WEDNESDAY

TO DO

_____

_____

○ THURSDAY

_____

_____

_____

_____

○ FRIDAY

_____

_____

_____

_____

○ SATURDAY / SUNDAY

_____

_____

_____

Month/Year: _____

__ Plan Your Day
__ Personal
__ Exercise
__ Spiritual
__ Family
__ Financial
__ Evaluate Your Day

_____TO_____

○ MONDAY

PRIORITIES

_____

○ TUESDAY

○ WEDNESDAY

TO DO

_____

○ THURSDAY

○ FRIDAY

○ SATURDAY / SUNDAY

Month/Year: _____

__ Plan Your Day
__ Personal
__ Exercise
__ Spiritual
__ Family
__ Financial
__ Evaluate Your Day

_____TO_____

○ MONDAY

PRIORITIES

_____

_____

○ TUESDAY

_____

_____

_____

_____

○ WEDNESDAY

TO DO

_____

○ THURSDAY

_____

_____

_____

_____

○ FRIDAY

_____

_____

_____

○ SATURDAY / SUNDAY

_____

_____

_____

Month/Year: _____

__ Plan Your Day
__ Personal
__ Exercise
__ Spiritual
__ Family
__ Financial
__ Evaluate Your Day

_____TO_____

○ MONDAY

PRIORITIES

_____

_____

○ TUESDAY

_____

_____

_____

○ WEDNESDAY

TO DO

_____

○ THURSDAY

_____

_____

_____

_____

○ FRIDAY

_____

_____

_____

○ SATURDAY / SUNDAY

_____

_____

_____

_____

Month/Year: _____

_____TO_____

○ MONDAY

PRIORITIES

_____

_____

○ TUESDAY

_____

_____

_____

○ WEDNESDAY

TO DO

_____

○ THURSDAY

_____

_____

_____

_____

○ FRIDAY

_____

_____

_____

○ SATURDAY / SUNDAY

_____

_____

_____

Month/Year: _____

_____TO_____

○ MONDAY

PRIORITIES

_____

_____

○ TUESDAY

_____

_____

_____

_____

○ WEDNESDAY

TO DO

_____

_____

○ THURSDAY

_____

_____

_____

_____

○ FRIDAY

_____

_____

_____

_____

○ SATURDAY / SUNDAY

_____

_____

_____

Month/Year: _____

__ Plan Your Day
__ Personal
__ Exercise
__ Spiritual
__ Family
__ Financial
__ Evaluate Your Day

_____TO_____

○ MONDAY

PRIORITIES

_____

_____

○ TUESDAY

_____

_____

_____

_____

○ WEDNESDAY

TO DO

_____

_____

○ THURSDAY

_____

_____

_____

_____

○ FRIDAY

_____

_____

_____

○ SATURDAY / SUNDAY

_____

_____

_____

_____

Month/Year: _____

_____TO_____

○ MONDAY

PRIORITIES

_____

○ TUESDAY

_____

○ WEDNESDAY

TO DO

_____

○ THURSDAY

_____

○ FRIDAY

_____

○ SATURDAY / SUNDAY

_____

Month/Year: _____

__ Plan Your Day
__ Personal
__ Exercise
__ Spiritual
__ Family
__ Financial
__ Evaluate Your Day

_____TO_____

○ MONDAY

PRIORITIES

_____

○ TUESDAY

○ WEDNESDAY

TO DO

○ THURSDAY

○ FRIDAY

○ SATURDAY / SUNDAY

Month/Year: _____

__ Plan Your Day
__ Personal
__ Exercise
__ Spiritual
__ Family
__ Financial
__ Evaluate Your Day

_____TO_____

○ MONDAY

PRIORITIES

_____

_____

○ TUESDAY

_____

_____

_____

_____

○ WEDNESDAY

TO DO

_____

_____

○ THURSDAY

_____

_____

_____

_____

○ FRIDAY

_____

_____

_____

_____

○ SATURDAY / SUNDAY

_____

_____

_____

_____

Month/Year: _____

_____TO_____

○ MONDAY

PRIORITIES

_____

_____

○ TUESDAY

_____

_____

_____

_____

○ WEDNESDAY

TO DO

_____

_____

○ THURSDAY

_____

_____

_____

_____

○ FRIDAY

_____

_____

_____

_____

○ SATURDAY / SUNDAY

_____

_____

_____

Month/Year: _____

_____TO_____

○ MONDAY

PRIORITIES

_____

○ TUESDAY

_____

○ WEDNESDAY

TO DO

_____

○ THURSDAY

_____

○ FRIDAY

_____

○ SATURDAY / SUNDAY

_____

Month/Year: _____ _____

_____TO_____

○ MONDAY

PRIORITIES

_____

_____

_____

○ TUESDAY

_____

_____

_____

_____

○ WEDNESDAY

TO DO

_____

_____

○ THURSDAY

_____

_____

_____

_____

○ FRIDAY

_____

_____

_____

○ SATURDAY / SUNDAY

_____

_____

_____

Month/Year: _____

__ Plan Your Day
__ Personal
__ Exercise
__ Spiritual
__ Family
__ Financial
__ Evaluate Your Day

_____TO_____

○ MONDAY

PRIORITIES

_____

_____

○ TUESDAY

_____

_____

_____

_____

○ WEDNESDAY

TO DO

_____

_____

○ THURSDAY

_____

_____

_____

_____

○ FRIDAY

_____

_____

_____

_____

○ SATURDAY / SUNDAY

_____

_____

_____

Month/Year: _____

_____TO_____

__ Plan Your Day
__ Personal
__ Exercise
__ Spiritual
__ Family
__ Financial
__ Evaluate Your Day

○ MONDAY

_____

○ TUESDAY

_____

○ WEDNESDAY

_____

○ THURSDAY

_____

○ FRIDAY

_____

○ SATURDAY / SUNDAY

_____

PRIORITIES

_____
_____
_____
_____
_____
_____

TO DO

_____
_____
_____
_____
_____
_____
_____
_____
_____
_____
_____
_____

Month/Year: _____

_____TO_____

○ MONDAY

PRIORITIES

_____

_____

○ TUESDAY

_____

_____

_____

_____

○ WEDNESDAY

TO DO

_____

_____

○ THURSDAY

_____

_____

_____

_____

_____

○ FRIDAY

_____

_____

_____

_____

○ SATURDAY / SUNDAY

_____

_____

_____

_____

Month/Year: _____

__ Plan Your Day
__ Personal
__ Exercise
__ Spiritual
__ Family
__ Financial
__ Evaluate Your Day

_____TO_____

○ MONDAY

PRIORITIES

_____

_____

○ TUESDAY

_____

_____

_____

_____

○ WEDNESDAY

TO DO

_____

○ THURSDAY

_____

_____

_____

_____

○ FRIDAY

_____

_____

_____

○ SATURDAY / SUNDAY

_____

_____

_____

Month/Year: _____

_____TO_____

○ MONDAY

PRIORITIES

_____

_____

○ TUESDAY

_____

_____

_____

_____

○ WEDNESDAY

TO DO

_____

_____

○ THURSDAY

_____

_____

_____

_____

○ FRIDAY

_____

_____

_____

_____

○ SATURDAY / SUNDAY

_____

_____

_____

_____

Month/Year: _____

__ Plan Your Day
__ Personal
__ Exercise
__ Spiritual
__ Family
__ Financial
__ Evaluate Your Day

_____TO_____

○ MONDAY

PRIORITIES

_____

○ TUESDAY

_____

○ WEDNESDAY

TO DO

_____

○ THURSDAY

_____

○ FRIDAY

_____

○ SATURDAY / SUNDAY

_____

Month/Year: _____

_____TO_____

○ MONDAY

PRIORITIES

_____

_____

○ TUESDAY

_____

_____

_____

○ WEDNESDAY

TO DO

_____

○ THURSDAY

_____

_____

_____

_____

○ FRIDAY

_____

_____

_____

_____

○ SATURDAY / SUNDAY

_____

_____

_____

Month/Year: _____

__ Plan Your Day
__ Personal
__ Exercise
__ Spiritual
__ Family
__ Financial
__ Evaluate Your Day

_____TO_____

○ MONDAY

PRIORITIES

_____

_____

○ TUESDAY

_____

_____

_____

_____

_____

○ WEDNESDAY

TO DO

_____

_____

○ THURSDAY

_____

_____

_____

_____

○ FRIDAY

_____

_____

_____

_____

○ SATURDAY / SUNDAY

_____

_____

_____

Month/Year: _____

_____TO_____

○ MONDAY

PRIORITIES

_____

_____

○ TUESDAY

_____

_____

_____

_____

○ WEDNESDAY

TO DO

_____

_____

○ THURSDAY

_____

_____

_____

_____

_____

○ FRIDAY

_____

_____

_____

_____

_____

○ SATURDAY / SUNDAY

_____

_____

_____

_____

Month/Year: _____

___ Plan Your Day
___ Personal
___ Exercise
___ Spiritual
___ Family
___ Financial
___ Evaluate Your Day

_____TO_____

○ MONDAY

PRIORITIES

_____

_____

_____

○ TUESDAY

_____

_____

_____

_____

_____

○ WEDNESDAY

TO DO

_____

_____

_____

○ THURSDAY

_____

_____

_____

_____

○ FRIDAY

_____

_____

_____

○ SATURDAY / SUNDAY

_____

_____

_____

Month/Year: _____

_____TO_____

○ MONDAY

PRIORITIES

_____

_____

○ TUESDAY

_____

_____

_____

_____

○ WEDNESDAY

TO DO

_____

_____

○ THURSDAY

_____

_____

_____

_____

_____

○ FRIDAY

_____

_____

_____

_____

_____

○ SATURDAY / SUNDAY

_____

_____

_____

_____

Month/Year: _____

__ Plan Your Day
__ Personal
__ Exercise
__ Spiritual
__ Family
__ Financial
__ Evaluate Your Day

_____TO_____

○ MONDAY

PRIORITIES

_____

○ TUESDAY

_____

○ WEDNESDAY

TO DO

_____

○ THURSDAY

_____

○ FRIDAY

_____

○ SATURDAY / SUNDAY

_____

Month/Year: _____

_____TO_____

○ MONDAY

PRIORITIES

_____

○ TUESDAY

○ WEDNESDAY

TO DO

○ THURSDAY

○ FRIDAY

○ SATURDAY / SUNDAY

Month/Year: _____

_____TO_____

○ MONDAY

PRIORITIES

_____

○ TUESDAY

_____

○ WEDNESDAY

TO DO

_____

○ THURSDAY

_____

○ FRIDAY

_____

○ SATURDAY / SUNDAY

_____

Month/Year: _____

_____TO_____

○ MONDAY

PRIORITIES

○ TUESDAY

○ WEDNESDAY

TO DO

○ THURSDAY

○ FRIDAY

○ SATURDAY / SUNDAY

Month/Year: _____

__ Plan Your Day
__ Personal
__ Exercise
__ Spiritual
__ Family
__ Financial
__ Evaluate Your Day

_____TO_____

○ MONDAY

PRIORITIES

_____

_____

○ TUESDAY

_____

_____

_____

_____

_____

○ WEDNESDAY

TO DO

_____

_____

○ THURSDAY

_____

_____

_____

_____

○ FRIDAY

_____

_____

_____

_____

○ SATURDAY / SUNDAY

_____

_____

_____

Month/Year: _____

_____TO_____

○ MONDAY

PRIORITIES

_____

_____

○ TUESDAY

_____

_____

_____

○ WEDNESDAY

TO DO

_____

_____

○ THURSDAY

_____

_____

_____

_____

○ FRIDAY

_____

_____

_____

_____

○ SATURDAY / SUNDAY

_____

_____

_____

_____

Month/Year: _____

__ Plan Your Day
__ Personal
__ Exercise
__ Spiritual
__ Family
__ Financial
__ Evaluate Your Day

_____ TO _____

○ MONDAY

PRIORITIES

_____

_____

○ TUESDAY

_____

_____

_____

_____

○ WEDNESDAY

TO DO

_____

_____

○ THURSDAY

_____

_____

_____

_____

○ FRIDAY

_____

_____

_____

○ SATURDAY / SUNDAY

_____

_____

_____

Made in the USA
Middletown, DE
13 September 2021